Gods of World
MYTHOLOGY

Don Nardo

ReferencePoint
Press

San Diego, CA

About the Author

Classical historian and award-winning author Don Nardo has written numerous acclaimed volumes about ancient civilizations and peoples. They include more than two dozen overviews of the mythologies of the Sumerians, Babylonians, Egyptians, Greeks, Romans, Persians, Celts, and others. Nardo, who also composes and arranges orchestral music, lives with his wife, Christine, in Massachusetts.

© 2022 ReferencePoint Press, Inc.
Printed in the United States

For more information, contact:
ReferencePoint Press, Inc.
PO Box 27779
San Diego, CA 92198
www.ReferencePointPress.com

LIBRARY OF CONGRESS CATALOGING-IN-PUBLICATION DATA

Names: Nardo, Don, 1947- author.
Title: Gods of world mythology / by Don Nardo.
Description: San Diego, CA : ReferencePoint Press, Inc. 2022. | Includes
    bibliographical references and index.
Identifiers: LCCN 2020056607 (print) | LCCN 2020056608 (ebook) | ISBN
    9781678200824 (library binding) | ISBN 9781678200831 (ebook)
Subjects: LCSH: Gods. | Mythology.
Classification: LCC BL473 .N375 2022 (print) | LCC BL473 (ebook) | DDC
    398/.45--dc23
LC record available at https://lccn.loc.gov/2020056607
LC ebook record available at https://lccn.loc.gov/2020056608

Miraculous Births and Other World Myths

Mighty Zeus, exalted chief god of the ancient Greeks, awoke one morning with a splitting headache. Dragging himself out of bed in his gleaming palace atop towering Mount Olympus, he hoped he would soon feel better. But the pain only worsened, and when the other Olympian deities heard about his plight, they gathered around him, each offering to help in some way.

Eventually, the afflicted god, still accompanied by the other divinities, wandered out into the palace courtyard. There he suddenly stopped and with a loud bellow grasped his head, as if trying to keep it from exploding. Seconds later it did just that. His swelling noggin abruptly split open, and to the astonishment of the onlookers, a splendid adult female form arose from that breach. She was clad in full armor and carried a spear and shield. As the early Greek poet Hesiod put it, in this way "Zeus gave forth grey-eyed Athena, awe-inspiring goddess who causes the clamor of war and forcefully commands on the battlefield."[1]

The other gods were appropriately astounded by the spectacle. The most remarkable thing, they agreed, was that their leader had given birth to a daughter on his own, without the traditional coupling with a female. Zeus's wife, Hera, queen of the Greek gods, found this fact disturbing. Envious of her divine mate, not long afterward

she decided to enact a miraculous birth of her own. From one of her thighs she brought into the world a male deity—Hephaestus, who became the god of fire and the divine blacksmith and armor-maker of Olympus.

Numerous Common Mythical Themes

The stories of the miraculous beginnings of Athena and Hephaestus are fairly familiar to Americans and Europeans. This is because Greek mythology has long been one of the major literary underpinnings of Western (European-based) culture. What many people do not realize, however, is that very similar tales exist in the mythologies of cultures and peoples in other parts of Europe and around the globe.

In ancient Italy, for example, the Romans, who eventually conquered the Greeks, had a comparable myth. The goddess Juno, wife of the head Roman god, Jupiter, decided to create a child of her own without her husband's sexual input. With the aid of a magic flower, she proceeded to give birth to the war god Mars.

Another example comes from Central America, where the Aztec people arose and flourished completely independently of Europe and its traditions. In Aztec lore, the earth mother goddess Coatlicue found a ball of feathers and wore it in her belt; soon she was pregnant with a son, who became the war god

Huitzilopochtli. Moreover, in a stunning parallel with Athena's birth myth, he emerged from his mother's body as an adult and wearing full armor. Similar miraculous births of deities appear in the mythologies of the Norse, Chinese, and Egyptians, to name only a few.

This painting from an ancient Greek vase shows the war-goddess Athena, dressed in full armor, rising up from inside her father Zeus's head, while several other astonished gods look on.

Such tales constitute only one of numerous mythical themes woven into the cultural traditions of ancient peoples around the globe. The Aztec earth goddess Coatlicue, who birthed the deity Huitzilopochtli, was a case in point. Almost all world mythologies feature a maternal earth deity like her. The Greeks had Gaia, whom they viewed as a conscious embodiment of the solid ground beneath their feet. In a like manner, the Romans had Ceres; the Norse Sif; and the Chinese Houtu. Houtu was said to have rearranged massive amounts of soil and entire mountains in order to shape the course of the Yellow River, China's chief waterway.

Similarly, each pantheon, or group of gods worshipped by a people or nation, had a major deity in charge of justice. For the Babylonians in the ancient Middle East it was Marduk; for the Celts, who dwelled in central and northern Europe, that god was Lugh; for the Greeks it was Zeus; and for the Igbo (or Ibo), a prominent East African people, it was Chukwu. Other deities who represented common thematic strands running through most world mythologies included divine tricksters, creator gods, and love gods, among others.

A Global Quest for Origins

Looking at the many similarities among the gods and myths of past peoples around the globe, it is only natural to wonder how those parallels came about. A number of modern scholars have concluded that it did not happen merely by coincidence. The late renowned mythologist Joseph Campbell, for instance, suggested that each culture's myths were influenced to some degree by those of older cultures. Moreover, that process may have begun long before primitive hunter-gatherers settled down and erected the first villages and towns in the Middle East, China, India, and Egypt.

Respected modern mythologist E.J. Michael Witzel agrees. In his 2012 book *The Origins of the World's Mythologies*, he asks, "How could people from Iceland to Polynesia and Mexico agree on so many points?" After all, "they were not in direct contact, separated as they were from each other by tens of thousands of miles and by some 5,000 years in time."[2]

Witzel goes on to answer that question by arguing that a single, original mythology sprang up among the first humans as they emerged in eastern Africa tens of thousands of years ago. From there, he says, the initial tales were told and retold by the descendants of those early hunters as they left Africa and began their global migrations. The mythologies of the early Hindus, Greeks, Japanese, and Maya, Witzel explains, "have a common narrative structure." Furthermore, "a large number of present and past mythologies [go] way back to a single source, from which they have branched off in various directions."[3]

This is why, he proposes, the Greek Zeus, Norse Odin, and Ibo Chukwu are so much alike. These and their fellow deities continue to fascinate people today because they helped shape the first human civilizations. All of us sprang from those cultures, Witzel points out, and we all eagerly "share the same quest for our origins."[4]

Immortality and Power: The Greco-Roman Gods

Not long after the imposing Athena, goddess of war and wisdom, was born from the head of her father, Zeus, life on earth underwent a dramatic change. Zeus's trusted adviser, the god Prometheus, created humans and taught them how to use fire, which helped them build a thriving civilization. In the centuries that followed, Athena watched with fascination as the humans erected cities, including majestic Athens. Steadily, she grew to admire the Athenians and desired to become their local patron deity, or divine protector.

One thing stood in the goddess's way, however. Her uncle Poseidon, lord of the seas, wanted that role for himself. Hearing of this rivalry, Zeus suggested that his daughter and brother take part in a public contest, with Zeus as judge. Whichever deity provided Athens with the most useful gift would win the competition and become the city's patron.

Poseidon, wielding his three-pronged spear, the trident, arrived in Athens first and stood atop the city's central hill, the Acropolis. In the words of the ancient myth teller today called Pseudo-Apollodorus, "With a blow of his trident on the middle of the Acropolis, he produced a [freshwater stream]." Then Athena leapt onto the Acropolis. "Having called on [the city's king] to witness her act of taking possession, she planted an olive tree."[5]

Zeus carefully weighed the situation and decided that giving Athens its first olive tree was the most valuable of the two feats. So he chose Athena as the winner of the contest. Thereafter, she remained the Athenians' proud patron and bore the nickname Athena Polias, meaning "Athena of the City."

The Power to Destroy Humankind

These events supposedly took place far back in the mists of time, long before the emergence of the so-called classical Greeks, who in the fifth century BCE created the world's first democracy and erected the magnificent Parthenon temple atop the Acropolis. The classical Greeks envisioned their gods as looking and acting like people. Yet no matter how much the gods resembled humans, the Greeks recognized two special differences. First, the gods were immortal, whereas people were born, grew old, and died.

The second factor that separated the gods from their human worshippers was the tremendous power those divinities wielded. As the classical Greek poet Pindar put it, "Single is the race . . . of men and gods. From a single mother we both draw breath. But a difference of power in everything keeps us apart."[6] It was understood, therefore, that the gods could easily destroy humanity if they chose to.

That divine power was a prominent theme running throughout the colorful stories making up Greek mythology. Although Poseidon lost the contest on the Acropolis to his niece, for instance, he

Odysseus
The king of the Greek island kingdom of Ithaca

successfully exerted his tremendous strength in numerous other tales. One of the more famous examples was his manipulation of the Greek king Odysseus. After helping other Greek leaders capture the city of Troy in Anatolia (today Turkey), Odysseus and his followers departed for home. But a massive storm scattered their ships. They ended up on a remote island inhabited by giant one-eyed creatures—the Cyclopes. During their escape, the Greeks blinded a Cyclops, who, to their horror, they later learned was Poseidon's son. The enraged god thereafter used his immense power to punish Odysseus repeatedly and kept him from returning to Greece for ten long years.

When Gods Lost Their Tempers

Meanwhile, Athena often employed her own considerable power to keep selected humans in line. Entering a contest with her divine uncle was acceptable to the goddess, but she viewed competing with a mere human as an insult. So when a woman named Arachne challenged Athena to see which of the two was the more talented weaver, the goddess lost her temper. Athena turned the maiden into a spider (which explains why modern scientists call spiders arachnids.)

Zeus, who had chosen his daughter as winner of the competition in Athens, possessed far more power than either Athena or Poseidon and wielded it frequently. One of the more famous examples of Zeus's legendary wrath was his punishment of his own adviser, Prometheus. The trouble between the two deities stemmed from Prometheus's gift of fire to humans. Earlier, Zeus had prohibited anyone from doing that, saying that only the immortal gods should benefit from fire.

Prometheus

The god who created humans and later gave them fire

But Prometheus pitied the beings he had created, who, lacking fire, could not cook their food. So he swiped some fire from the gods' hearth on Mount Olympus and presented it to the humans. "He showed them how to cook and how to keep themselves warm," the late modern myth teller W.H.D. Rouse wrote. With fire, they also learned "how to make bricks and burn pottery [and] how to smelt metals and make tools."[7]

When Zeus found out what had happened, he was livid. The most powerful of the Olympian immortals proceeded to inflict a

Nineteenth-century German artist Alexander Zick created this dramatic painting of Prometheus's agonizing daily punishment, an ordeal ordered by his former mentor, mighty Zeus.

horrifying punishment on his former adviser. Prometheus was chained to the summit of a faraway mountain, and there each day a giant vulture tore out the captive's liver. Then each night the organ grew back and the grisly process continued to repeat itself.

The Romans Overhaul Their Pantheon

Such stories describing Zeus, Athena, and other powerful Greek gods steadily became known all across the ancient Mediterranean world. Among the many peoples who heard them were the Romans, who rose to prominence in Italy. The Greek deities and their colorful tales turned out to be particularly fascinating to Rome's residents, in part because of the way the Romans initially viewed their own early gods. Before they came into close contact with Greek civilization in the last few centuries BCE, the Romans recognized simple, mostly formless nature spirits called numina. Each numen exerted influence over only a small, localized aspect of life. Flora, for instance, made flowers grow, Sylvanus protected woodcutters, and Janus guarded doorways.

Unlike the Greek gods, most numina were not very powerful, although there were a few exceptions. For instance, the Romans had a story about a feat performed by Janus when, in the dim past, an enemy people attacked Rome. The invaders attempted to pass through a gate that led to the main town square. Because a gate is a kind of doorway, Janus held sway there, and he made the attackers pay dearly. According to the first-century-BCE Roman poet Ovid, the deity forced water from some local fountains to spurt out in "a sudden gush." Janus also injected hot "sulfur into the water channels, so that the boiling liquid might bar the way against [the invaders]."[8]

Such displays of power were rare among the numina, who were not nearly as strong as Zeus and his Olympians. Along with the Greek gods' colorful personalities, this made these divinities very attractive to the Romans. So as the latter conquered the Greek lands and steadily absorbed Greek cultural ideas, they began to associate some of their numina with the more formidable Greek gods. In early Roman society, for example, Jupiter had been a simple sky spirit with modest powers. In Rome's overhauled pantheon, however, he was equated with the leading Greek deity, Zeus. Similarly, the humble Roman farming spirit Mars became the equivalent of the Greek war god Ares.

The Divine Stars of the Story

The Romans also absorbed the myths associated with the Greek divinities, so that, for instance, Jupiter inherited most of Zeus's

Athena's Birth Myth Captured in Art

Several ancient writers described the myth in which Athena sprang miraculously from her father's head. Of those literary accounts, the most often cited is the one penned by the seventh-century-BCE epic poet Hesiod in his *Theogony*. Greek painters and other artists also depicted the events of that tale, but most of those artworks long ago decayed and disappeared. Fortunately, the third-century-CE Greek orator Philostratus of Lemnos viewed and described in writing a now-lost painting of Athena's birth that was once on display in western Italy. According to Philostratus, the painting showed a crowd of deities gathered around their leader, Zeus. Those onlookers

> shudder at the sight of Athena, who at this moment has just burst forth fully armed from the head of Zeus. [As] for the material of her panoply [armor and weapons], no one could guess it; for as many as are the colors of the rainbow [are] the colors of her armor. Hephaestus seems at a loss to know [how] her armor was born with her. Zeus breathes deeply with delight, like men who have undergone a great contest for a great prize, and he looks searchingly for his daughter, feeling pride in his offspring.

Philostratus the Elder, *Imagines*, trans. Arthur Fairbanks. Cambridge, MA: Harvard University Press, 1931, pp. 245, 247.

legends. Yet Roman writers did assign some new myths to their refurbished, more awe-inspiring gods. Often this was meant to justify Rome's rapid conquest of the known world. Such new Roman myths claimed that the gods had chosen the Romans to rule humanity forever, a destiny vividly described in the *Aeneid*. Penned by Ovid's contemporary, Virgil, it instantly became Rome's cherished national epic.

Many gods appear in the myths constituting that massive work, but Jupiter and his mate Juno are the divine stars of the story. In that tale, they both watched the Greek siege of Troy with great interest and noticed that

Juno
Jupiter's divine wife and a protector of women

when the city eventually fell, a Trojan prince, Aeneas, escaped. Jupiter decided to give that young man a fateful mission. Aeneas and his small band of followers were to sail to Italy and there establish the Roman race. In so doing, Jupiter said, they would fulfill an ancient prophecy foretelling that Rome would someday rule the world.

To ensure that destiny came to pass, the chief god repeatedly aided Aeneas. When a fire was about to engulf the Trojan ships, for example, Jupiter whipped up a huge rainstorm that rapidly

A medieval Spanish painting depicts the scene from Virgil's Aeneid *in which the goddess Juno asks the god of the winds to blow up a storm and thereby wreck the hero Aeneas's ships.*

Vesta and Female Chastity

In part because the Roman goddess Vesta was a virgin, she demanded that her priestesses—the renowned Vestal Virgins—be chaste, too. She and her myths, which dealt mainly with her purity, strongly influenced Roman social customs. Young Roman women were expected to refrain from sexual activities before marriage. The Romans believed that the purity Vesta promoted by example was a virtue that would benefit society as a whole. The reasoning behind that belief was built around a concept called *pudicita*, loosely defined as "sexual loyalty" for the good of the Roman state. It was thought that when a young woman maintained sexual loyalty to her husband, and *only* her husband, the couple's fertility, or chances of producing healthy children, would be significantly enhanced. That supposedly made Rome stronger and ensured both its survival and longevity. People commonly viewed society and the Roman state as the sum total of many patriotic families working together for the mutual good of all. Thus, just as it was seen as patriotic for young men to serve in the military and defend the state, it was equally patriotic for young women to be sexually loyal.

doused the flames. What frustrated both Jupiter and Aeneas, however, was that Juno opposed the Trojan expedition. She wanted her favorite city, Carthage (in North Africa), and not Rome, to end up achieving world dominance. Time after time, therefore, she tried to impede Aeneas's progress.

Predictably, Juno was furious when the Trojans landed in western Italy. Soon afterward, when Aeneas sailed northward to the future site of Rome, the irate goddess sent Alecto, the flying spirit of anger, to sow hatred between the newcomers and local Latin-speaking tribes. Such efforts to stir up trouble ultimately failed, however. Aeneas soon married a Latin princess, Lavinia, and the couple founded the city of Lavinium, named for her. Over time, the union of the Latin and Trojan peoples gave rise to a new and supremely noble race—the Romans. In triumph, mighty Jupiter announced that he hereby granted the Romans "dominion without end." They were, he ordained, "the master race, the wearers of the toga. So it is willed!"[9]

A Love of Grace and Purity

Just as the Greeks admired the great power wielded by their gods, the Romans revered Jupiter, Juno, and many other divine beings for the same reason. Yet there was one deity whom the Romans respected not for her power but for her grace and purity. She was Vesta, the virgin goddess of hearths. Her domain included hearths in family homes and in her temple in Rome. There her priestesses, known as the Vestal Virgins, maintained her sacred fire.

In her best-known myth, Vesta, along with most of the gods and nature spirits, attended a large party. Partway through the festivities she grew tired, went to an empty room, and fell asleep. Soon the mischievous spirit Priapus appeared and, seeing that Vesta was vulnerable, decided to take advantage of the situation. He tried to sneak up on her, Ovid wrote, and "walked on tiptoe with throbbing heart."[10] At the last second, however, a donkey brayed in the distance, which awakened the goddess. She was able to stop Priapus and to maintain her virginity, for the sake of herself and all Romans; that purity, noted scholar Jane F. Gardner points out, "was at once the symbol and the guarantee of the welfare of Rome."[11]

Trade-Offs and Tragedy: The Norse Gods

Odin, leader of the Norse gods, whom the Norse often called the "All-Father," approached a grove of tall trees, the branches of which shaded a strangely dark-colored pool of water. The latter he knew was a magical well overseen by a secretive, rarely seen supernatural being named Mimir. Odin had undertaken several quests for knowledge in his long life-time. Each quest had made him wiser and more enlightened about the universe shared by the gods, humans, and a scary array of giants, dragons, and other monstrous creatures.

No matter how knowledgeable Odin became, however, he had heard that one entity was wiser than he. It was Mimir, who was said to have acquired enormous amounts of knowledge by drinking from the murky depths of the pool that Odin now stood beside. According to legend, it was called *Mimisbrunnr*, meaning "Mimir's Well."

It was also rumored that no one else could sip from those inky waters without Mimir's permission. So Odin called out to the pool's guardian spirit and requested the privilege of tasting some of the precious liquid. In a deep-toned reply, Mimir warned the god that permission would come at a very steep, unpleasant price—the sacrifice of one of Odin's eyes. The All-Father considered the offer for a moment and made up his mind. Pulling a dagger from his belt, he reached up and used the blade to pop out his right eye, which he speedily threw into the gloomy pool. Just as swiftly, Mimir kept his side of the grisly bargain by filling a drinking horn with water from the well and handing it to Odin, who guzzled it. According to Stockholm University professor Christian Christensen, the large mass of knowledge drawn from the magical pool transformed Odin into "the wisest among all Norse gods. It is said that what [he] sought by drinking water from Mimir's well and gained by sacrificing his eye was not knowledge in an academic or scholarly sense, but rather, enlightenment and illumination in an ethereal [other-worldly] and spiritual way."[12] An important theme of that famous Norse myth is that the quest for enlightenment is an exceedingly noble aim, which made Odin himself a morally upright character.

Haunted by a Dark Shadow

The story of Odin's trade of his precious eye for equally precious knowledge also illustrates one of the most profound themes associated with the Norse gods and their world: that life is filled with trade-offs and sacrifices. Moreover, those trade-offs can often be harsh or tragic, not only for human beings, but also for the gods themselves. This idea that tragedy might strike a person or deity at any time strongly pervaded Norse mythology. It was a dark, bleak theme, a sort of foreboding shadow that consistently haunted Odin and the other gods. In most of the mystical tales told by the Norse, the gods do manage to win over their opponents in the short run. But these victories are rendered meaningless in the long run, for in looking at the stories in the collective sense, it is clear that the gods ultimately have no chance of overcoming the forces of evil and chaos.

This concept of ultimate tragedy is the central theme and focus of one of the chief myths about the Norse gods. In that scenario, fate decided long ago, when the universe was still young, that in the far future there would come Ragnarok, the "Twilight of

Odin, chief of the Norse gods, brandishes his formidable sword in this medieval ink-on-paper rendering. The artist included the detail of the god's missing eye, lost in the encounter with Mimir.

the Gods." In this final fight between the gods and their ghastly enemies, the gods lost. In the words of the great modern mythologist Edith Hamilton, the Norse deities' home, the fortress-like Asgard, "is a grave and solemn place, over which hangs the threat of an inevitable doom. The gods know that a day will come when they will be destroyed [and] Asgard will fall in ruins. The cause the forces of good are fighting to defend against the forces of evil is hopeless. Nevertheless, the gods will fight for it to the end. Necessarily, the same is true of humanity."[13]

Indeed, during Ragnarok humans fought alongside the gods, and many people perished with them, leaving the universe in the

The Bleakness of Norse Life

The bleak and isolated lives of ancient Norse peoples helped shape their unique deities. The desolate, discouraging outlook pervading Norse religion—based on the prophecy of Ragnarok and its associated myths—may have come partly from the fact that the Norse themselves frequently endured deprivation and dreary lives. They dwelled in Europe's cold and sparsely populated far northern regions, including Scandinavia and later Iceland and other islands of the cold northern seas. They endured long, sometimes punishing winters, and crop-growing seasons were short, often making food scarce. Thus, life was a persistent struggle for existence, which tended to toughen people. In the words of an expert on Norse lore, H.R. Ellis Davidson:

> They were very conscious of the grim underworld where giants and monsters dwelt, and of the constant threat to their precarious little world once the forces of chaos were unleashed. Their experience of a savage world in which kingdoms were constantly set up and destroyed, with a background of stormy seas and long cold winter nights, gave a somber tinge to their picture of the realm of the gods, but also imparted a sturdy vigor to the figures who people their myths.

H.R. Ellis Davidson, *Scandinavian Mythology*. New York: Peter Bedrick, 1986, p. 8.

control of the evil ones. Odin knew that would happen—that in the end fate would in a real way demand a tragic outcome—which explains why he was so often such a sad and gloomy figure. "He knew the bleak future for the gods and humans and it weighed heavy on him," Hamilton pointed out. He felt it was his solemn responsibility to do his best to postpone the ultimate day of doom. "In large part, that is why he constantly sought more wisdom. Perhaps, in the hidden corridors of his mind, he hoped that he might discover some shred of knowledge that might change that terrible future for the better."[14]

Binding the Giant Wolf

Meanwhile, Odin reasoned, one way to buy time for the doomed gods and humans was to destroy as many of the world's dark forces as possible. This is why he became an accomplished monster fighter. Many of the creatures he battled were the offspring of Loki, who in some medieval sources was

called a fire god but who was better known as the trickster god. The term *trickster* was meant to describe his shifty nature, both physically and verbally. Physically he was a shape-shifter who could instantly change into a fish, bird, giant, or even a puff of smoke. Loki's shiftiness could also be seen in the realm of the spoken word. He was a master of turning truth into lies. He lied so often that he was sometimes called the unflattering title "Father of Lies."

Sometimes Loki worked with and for Odin and the other gods. But other times he worked against them. One of the chief ways he made life hard for them was to sire several monstrous, troublemaking children. Faced with those vicious offspring, Odin,

his wife Frigg, their son Balder (god of wisdom), the war god Tyr, the sky god Thor, and other deities felt they could not stand idly by. Frequently, they felt compelled to battle the repulsive members of Loki's brood in order to save humanity.

One of the more memorable examples of these heroic efforts was when the rugged residents of Asgard dealt with one of Loki's most dangerous children, the huge and incredibly vicious wolf Fenrir. Odin sensed that this horrible creature might be potentially the most treacherous monster in the entire universe. Confirming that suspicion, one of the Norns, a group of female spirits who could predict future events, told the gods that Fenrir was a serious threat to humanity's survival. Odin gave the matter some thought and decided on the most effective way to render the great beast harmless. He ordered the other gods to capture Fenrir, securely bind him, and bring him to Asgard, where the divine beings could keep a round-the-clock watch over him.

The problem was that the giant wolf was enormously strong and thereby able to break every chain the gods employed to hold

Fenrir
A vicious giant wolf and one of Loki's offspring

him. Desperate, Odin approached some dwarfs known for their magical spells. As modern myth teller Neil Philip tells it, "They made a fetter [chain] called Gleipnir. Silky soft, Gleipnir was made of special ingredients: the sound of a cat's footfall; a woman's beard; a mountain's roots; a bear's sinews [strength]; a fish's breath; and a bird's spittle."[15]

When Fenrir first gazed on the chain made from these seemingly formless materials, he laughed aloud and bragged that nothing so flimsy could hold him. But when the war god Tyr slipped the new chain around the beast, it held him tight and he could not escape. "Furious," Philip continues, Fenrir "clamped its great jaws together and bit off the god Tyr's right hand."[16]

A color lithograph depicts the famous myth in which Tyr and other leading Norse gods attempt to bind the monstrous wolf Fenrir. Tyr lost his right hand in the incident.

The Repulsive Yet Resilient Hel

Of Loki's malignant offspring, perhaps the most repulsive was Hel. According to Daniel McCoy, an American scholar of Norse religion, that female creature was "a giantess and/or goddess who rules over the identically-named Hel, the underworld where many of the dead dwell. Her name's meaning of 'Hidden' surely has to do with the underworld and the dead being 'hidden' or buried beneath the ground."

A number of Scandinavian myths call Hel the queen of the dead. They describe her upper body as that of a normal woman and her lower body as black and rotten looking. Odin, Thor, and the other gods were at first unsure about how to deal with her. Eventually, they agreed to toss her into the depths of Niflheim, a desolate, frozen land where no living plants or animals dwelled. Odin himself did the honors. He and the others assumed that Hel would thereafter be powerless and that humanity would forget she had ever existed. But they were mistaken. She not only survived, but once in Niflheim she made it a haven for dead souls. In the centuries that followed, she waited patiently for the advent of Ragnarok, in which she hoped to, and indeed did, get her revenge on the gods.

Daniel McCoy, "Hel (Goddess)," Norse Mythology for Smart People. https://norse-mythology.org.

When the Sun Turned Black

All the deities of Asgard expressed their sympathies for Tyr's nasty disfigurement. But he recognized that this was merely one of life's sometimes unpleasant trade-offs. It was indeed a small price to pay for saving the universe, at least temporarily, from a horrifying monster.

Even the dishonest Loki accepted that now and then he must sacrifice by compromising with the other gods in order to further his own aims. One such episode was the time that a deformed giant named Thiazi threatened to kill Loki if the trickster did not deliver to him Idun, the goddess who caused the rejuvenation of plants in the spring. Loki did so. But then Odin and Thor promised to destroy Loki if he did not reverse himself and liberate Idun. To accomplish that rescue, Loki took on the shape of a falcon, scooped Idun up in his talons, and flew her back to Asgard. Thiazi pursued them, but when the towering creature approached

Idun
The Norse goddess who oversaw the rejuvenation of plants each spring

the gods' stronghold, they created a wall of fire that burned him to death.

Loki's supposed good deed in this case was enacted to rectify a problem that he himself had created when he led Idun to the giant. Deception and trouble were as much a part of Loki as the constant quest for knowledge was a part of Odin. Moreover, part of the ultimate tragedy of the Norse gods was that they continually gave him the benefit of the doubt, perhaps hoping he would eventually reform himself.

Loki did quite the opposite, however. In the end, when the catastrophe of Ragnarok finally came, he helped the forces of evil defeat his fellow deities. The gods' valiant last stand was partially described in an old Scandinavian poem, *Voluspo*. "The sun turns black," it states, and "earth sinks in the sea; the hot stars down from heaven are whirled; fierce grows the steam and the life-feeding flame, till fire leaps high about heaven itself."[17]

A few other Norse myths present different outcomes for Ragnarok. In one, all the gods and humans perished and the world turned dark and lifeless until a new sun appeared in the sky and a new race of humans appeared. A second story claimed that a handful of minor gods managed to survive the disaster and rebuilt the world. Still another tale said that no gods survived but that two humans did—a man, Lif, and a woman, Lofthrasir—and they proceeded to repopulate the world. One thing these myths all have in common is that the great gods of old—Odin, Tyr, Thor, and their brethren—were destroyed. And with them departed a superb blend of heroism, nobility, decency, and honor that to this day has never been replicated.

Eternity and Endless Cycles: The Hindu Gods

Brahma suddenly opened his eyes, having awakened from what seemed like a long and now distant and mysterious dream. In some ways he looked human, or more precisely like four humans, for he had four heads, each with two eyes, a nose, and a mouth. He also had four arms. Thus, he was humanlike, yet *not* human. In fact, he was a divine being, and he fully sensed that strange reality as he surveyed his surroundings. In all directions there stretched a dimly lit, apparently limitless sea that seemed to have no shores, no bottom, and no life beyond himself.

Although Brahma floated in the midst of that dark, foreboding ocean, he felt no fear of drowning because, being a god, he was immune to ordinary death. He also sensed that deep within himself he held a vast amount of knowledge—some form of universal wisdom. Later, the ancient Hindus would honor him with a hymn, calling him "the sole image of wisdom," and add that he was "one, permanent, pure, immovable, the everlasting seer [wise one] of all things."[18]

An undetermined span of time passed, and Brahma slowly rose to the water's surface. It was then that he realized he was enveloped by the petals of a huge lotus flower that rested on a small piece of dry land. Stepping from the lotus onto the ground, he looked out at the sea and caught sight of a big snake approaching. As the serpent reached the clump of land, Brahma could see a living form resting within its coils. In some way—and for the moment he had no idea how—he knew that the sleeping form was also divine and that his name was Vishnu.

Mere seconds after recognizing the slumbering fellow god, Brahma heard a rhythmic sound echoing from the sea's depths— a repeated chanting of the syllable *om*. It grew louder and louder until it made the vast sea tremble, and Vishnu awakened with a start. At that same instant, the sun appeared on the horizon, signaling the first dawn. The two gods then greeted each other and began to create a world containing continents, mountains, forests, animals, and people.

Numerous Divine Avatars

In that story—one of several creation tales within Hindu mythology—Vishnu's awakening did not cause the first dawn ever. Rather, it was the sun's first appearance in the newest of many identical first dawns, each part of a new beginning of the world. In fact, that repeating cycle was, and in Hindu lore remains, endless. Early Hindus believed, and many modern Hindus still hold, that the universe and time itself are eternal and therefore have no set beginning or end. Instead, in each new cycle the gods and human society arise, thrive, and eventually decline and disappear, which in turn leads to the next creation cycle.

As for how long each cycle lasts, no one knows for sure. But most Hindu philosophers and mythologists think that a single cycle can be many billions of years long. Such a time span breaks down into several smaller subcycles, the most basic of which is called a *kalpa*. According to English mythologist Veronica Ions, a *kalpa* is "one mere day in the life of Brahma [within a given cycle]

A decoration from the magnificent Hindu temple in Mayapur, in eastern India, shows the god Brahma sitting within the petals of the large lotus flower described in the Hindu myth of creation.

but is equivalent to 4.32 billion years on earth. When Brahma wakes, the three worlds (heavens, middle, and lower regions) are created, and when he sleeps, they are reduced to chaos."[19]

Another cornerstone of Hindu mythology and philosophy is that the gods Brahma, Vishnu, and their fellow deity Shiva together make up a sacred divine trinity (the Trimurti). Furthermore, although they and other Hindu gods appear in the myths as separate beings with distinct characters and abilities, they are in reality disguises, or avatars, of a single, all-powerful being—Brahman (not to be confused with his avatar Brahma).

A Struggle Never Before Seen

Among the numerous divine manifestations of Brahman, perhaps the most beloved are the avatars of Vishnu, the universe's protector, or preserver. In that capacity, he often accomplished heroic feats intended to destroy demons and other evil forces. Supposedly, he visited earth frequently—at least once in each repeating cycle—and during each visit he wore a different disguise.

Ravana
King of the demon
kingdom of Lanka

Of those diverse avatars, the seventh one, Rama, was said to have been particularly brave and to have performed many courageous deeds. Good-looking and muscular, he was also a skilled military leader, which came in handy when humanity was threatened by the hideous and powerful demon Ravana. That fearsome fiend ruled the cursed kingdom of Lanka and raised an army of tens of thousands of demons and other monstrous creatures.

Bent on destroying Ravana's forces, Rama's army of humans and gods marched on and attacked Lanka. A bloody battle ensued, in which large numbers of demons were slaughtered. Fuming with anger, Ravana decided to kill his hated enemy, Rama, and himself. To that end the demon king challenged the young man to single combat. The fight that followed is described in the ancient Indian epic poem the *Ramayana*. When Rama and Ravana tangled, it states, it was "a struggle as had never been seen on earth." Both warriors "were skilled archers, both knew all the science of warfare, both had weapons made by the high gods, and neither had ever known defeat."[20]

The evil Ravana fought well, but it was not enough to withstand the powers and skills of one of the greatest of all divine beings. During an awe-inspiring charge, Rama knocked the demon from his chariot and proceeded to slice his broken body to shreds.

Valiant Krishna vs. Evil Keshi

The victorious Rama enjoyed several other adventures. Meanwhile, beneath his skin, the part of him who remained Vishnu kept in mind that earth, the gods, and humanity would later experience other cycles of birth, growth, demise, and rebirth. Moreover, in future cycles he would surely return in different avatars and face off against evil in various other forms.

This is exactly what happened. In a later universal cycle, Vishnu visited earth once more, this time in the guise of a new avatar, the hero Krishna. Ancient documents described him as an extremely

GODS AND CULTURE

The Hindu Epics and Indian Society

The Hindu myths differ from those of most other world mythologies because those stories are still part of a living culture, most of whose members dwell in India and nearby nations. Indeed, many of the major Hindu myths are regular features of modern Indian life and influence the way people think, worship, and entertain themselves. Among the most influential tales of that sort are the ones contained in two large-scale ancient literary works—the epic poems known as the *Ramayana* and the *Mahabharata*. The first, named for Vishnu's avatar Rama, features dozens of stories chronicling that heroic character's many adventures and battles with evil beings.

These stories still have strong appeal in modern Hindu culture. This was evident when a high-budget miniseries based on the *Ramayana* was shown on television for the first time in the early 1990s. During the hours when each episode aired, the streets of India's cities and larger towns, which are usually teeming with cars and crowds of pedestrians and bicycle riders, were nearly deserted. Hundreds of millions of people remained in front of their TV sets all through the lengthy broadcasts.

handsome young man with blue skin who was both fearless and multitalented. In the words of the popular modern Indian thinker and writer Sadhguru, Krishna was at times childlike. But he was also "a terrible prankster, an enchanting flute player, a graceful dancer, an irresistible lover, a truly valiant warrior, a ruthless vanquisher of his foes . . . [and] an astute statesman and kingmaker."[21]

One of the many foes that Krishna fought was the repulsive demon Keshi, who looked like a large, badly deformed horse with many long, sharp teeth. An evil king named Kamsa feared Krishna and commanded Keshi to track down and slay the blue-skinned youth.

Krishna
The eighth avatar of the preserver god Vishnu

After searching throughout northern India, Keshi found Krishna conversing with some young milkmaids in a farmer's field. Wasting no time, the horse-demon attacked, rushing straight at its prey at a full gallop. While the girls scattered to safety, Krishna, unafraid, stood his ground. At the last second he calmly sidestepped and tripped the monster, who toppled to the ground. Filled with rage, Keshi got up and attacked again. But Krishna was too quick and strong and easily tossed him around the field several times.

Finally, the furious demon opened its massive mouth and rushed straight at the young man, meaning to swallow him whole. As usual, however, Krishna stayed calm and this time rammed an arm into Keshi's mouth. That limb then rapidly expanded in size, first choking the demon and then tearing its jaws and head apart. As Keshi's lifeless remains crumpled into the grass, the young man smiled and went in search of his friends.

The valiant deity Rama (shooting the bow in the foreground), one of Vishnu's avatars, leads his forces in a furious battle against the evil demon Ravana (with the multiple heads at upper right).

Krishna and the Milkmaids

Embedded within the philosophical concept of endless cycles of time and alternate realities is the subtheme of multiplicity. A frequent feature of the Hindu myths, multiplicity most often shows up in those stories as a large number of seemingly identical or similar objects. Common, for instance, are supernatural beings—gods and monsters alike—having multiple arms.

Among the more charming examples are the tales of Vishnu's avatar Krishna and his friendships with a group of farmers' daughters, often referred to as milkmaids. Krishna sometimes went to dances with them. Initially, he did not want to be seen as playing favorites, so he grew dozens of extra arms. That way he could dance with all of the girls at the same time. In time, however, the young hero fell in love with the milkmaid Radha. While the other girls were disappointed not to be chosen, they were happy for the young couple. Sometimes they walked alongside the lovers during outings in the countryside. In such situations, Krishna exploited the theme of multiplicity in a different way. When the girls walked alongside him and Radha, he created numerous images of himself, each of which held a single girl's hand and made her feel safe and comfortable.

A Refreshing View of Reality

A crucial aspect of the alternate cycles of life recognized in Hindu lore is that each new cycle can be seen as a reality separate from the ones before and after it. Moreover, even within a given cycle, a unique and unexpected reality can result when a god cleverly introduces a surprising alternative way of looking at things. A famous tale of Ganesha, the god of knowledge and wisdom, illustrates this concept in a touching, somewhat playful way.

Ganesha, who had a human body but an elephant's head, rode everywhere atop a mouse. According to Indian writer Subhamoy Das, an expert on Hindu history and lore:

Each Hindu deity has a particular animal-vehicle, or *vahana*, on which it travels. The Sanskrit word translates literally as "that which carries," or "that which pulls." These vehicles, which are either animals or birds, represent the various spiritual and psychological forces that carry each deity and represent it. So important are the vahanas that [in Hindu art] deities are seldom depicted without their corresponding creatures.[22]

Ganesha
The elephant-headed god of knowledge and wisdom

One day Ganesha and his brother, the war god Karthikeya, had an argument. They had found a tasty mango in the forest, and each wanted it for himself. While they bickered, the destroyer god Shiva happened by and proposed a way to settle the dispute, namely a race around the world, the winner of which would have the mango for himself.

The two brothers agreed to the challenge, and Karthikeya jumped onto his *vahana*, a peacock, and swiftly flew away on his journey round the globe. That left Ganesha to ride his slowly crawling mouse. Clearly at a disadvantage, Ganesha had a brilliant idea. He directed the mouse to carry him around Shiva, a distance of only a few feet, and promptly declared himself the winner.

Puzzled, Shiva demanded an explanation. Ganesha replied, with a wry smile, that from his own humble and unique viewpoint, the mighty Shiva was his whole world. Both flattered and impressed by Ganesha's ingenious interpretation of reality, Shiva declared the elephant-headed deity the winner. In a universe filled with countless cycles and realities, Shiva said, Ganesha's shrewd and practical move was both acceptable and refreshing.

Jovial and colorful, the elephant-headed Ganesha, god of knowledge, rides atop his personal vahana *(animal vehicle), the trusted mouse Mooshika. The two went everywhere together.*

Foxes, Dogs, and Dragons: The Chinese Gods

Nuwa was well aware that she was a heavenly being. However, she was not at all certain where she had come from. As near as she could tell, she and several other Chinese gods had simply appeared out of nothingness high up in the sky. They were not the first of their kind. Indeed, as they gazed downward, they could see the first divinity—Pangu—who was still putting the finishing touches on the surface of the planet he had recently created.

Nuwa was also unsure why each deity looked either a little or a lot different from the others. Some had a head, two arms, and two legs—what in the future would come to be called humanlike. Other deities had four legs and fur, while still others had scaly skin and claws. Nuwa herself displayed a mix of features. Her upper body had a human head and two arms with smooth skin, but her lower body had scaly skin and two massive three-toed feet with sharp claws—a physical form that would later be called dragon-like.

While she pondered these seeming oddities, Nuwa considered for a moment what being a divine entity meant. Certainly, it entailed being immortal and possessing magical powers that allowed her to manipulate various natural elements. She also seemed to sense that part of the natural order for a deity was to have followers—lesser and mortal worshippers.

No such worshippers existed on earth yet. So Nuwa took the initiative and fashioned a race of them, creatures that became known as humans. She created them from the rich, moist soil lining the banks of China's Yellow River. At first she molded them one by one, but in time she accelerated the procedure by rubbing a long sheaf of sugar cane in the mud. In the words of University of Oxford scholar Tao Tao Liu Sanders, each time she shook the sheaf, hundreds of tiny clumps of soil fell off and swiftly "transformed into men and women." Over time, when Nuwa felt she had made enough humans on her own, she "instituted marriage among them so that they could procreate and continue the human race without any further help from her."[23]

> **Nuwa**
> A half-human half-dragon goddess who created humanity

The Fox Goddess and the Scholar

The stories making up Chinese mythology remain somewhat unclear about why Nuwa chose human form for her mortal creations. She could just as easily have made them look like dragons, dragon-human hybrids like herself, or other animals. What is more certain is that animals played a central role in the myths of early China. Not only did some gods take partial or full animal form, but also ordinary animals interacted closely with various deities. Moreover, those interactions frequently affected humans, their society, and even their destiny.

Of the many hundreds of Chinese myths that feature animal-shaped gods and spirts, a large proportion involve foxes. In fact, fox-like characters are featured in those ancient tales more often than any other type. Some were merely mischievous creatures who tricked or tormented humans. But a fair number were manifestations of the fox goddess Huxian. Her very name identified her to the ancient Chinese, because the root word *hu* meant

According to Chinese mythology, Pangu was the god of creation, as well as the first god ever to exist. In this lively modern pastel drawing, he separates earth below from the heavens above.

"fox," and the word *xian* meant "immortal." Hence, she was the "immortal fox."

In one of her best-known myths, Huxian came upon a handsome young scholar. She was attracted to him and so decided to take the form of a beautiful young woman named Hong-yu. The two spent the night together. The young man promptly fell in love with her, but as a divine being she did not desire a permanent relationship with a mere human, so she moved on.

Before doing so, however, she found a pretty young woman who agreed to marry him. Unfortunately for all involved, soon after the wedding a criminal kidnapped the new wife, and in despair she took her own life. Making matters worse, the local police did not know about the criminal and charged the scholar with his wife's death. When Hong-yu heard what had happened, she felt partly responsible and convinced the police that the young man was innocent. He was allowed to resume his life. Neither the scholar nor the police ever found out that the lovely Hong-yu was actually Huxian, a goddess who looked like a fox.

Huxian
A shape-shifting fox goddess

Ghost Month

Many of China's ancient myths have influenced modern Chinese culture. One example is Ghost Month. Celebrated annually throughout the country, it is based on a popular myth involving Yang-wang, the chief god of the underworld and afterlife. In that tale, he decided to take some time off to relax and gave the monstrous creatures that guarded the underworld's borders a brief vacation as well. In their absence, the souls of the dead escaped and wandered across earth's surface. Some paid visits to their still-living relatives and friends, while others aimlessly roamed the streets and forests. During that period, a large proportion of the risen ghosts terrified the living, played mischievous pranks, or both.

Based on that story, each year for two weeks during the seventh lunar month (which varies from year to year), the Chinese avidly pretend to appease the roaming spirits. In one of the more common Ghost Month customs, people set up tables in the streets and cover them with an array of fruits and other treats. Some folks also construct paper lanterns shaped like lotus flowers and throw the lanterns into rivers. Supposedly, as these objects float downstream, they show the spirits their way back to the land of the dead.

The Queen, the Dog, and the Princess

Another common animal in the mythology of China was the dog, a creature widely admired among the ancient Chinese. Sometimes a god or goddess took the form of a dog, while in other cases an actual dog was aided by a divine being's magical abilities. That second scenario is the premise of one of the most beloved of all Chinese myths—the story of Panhu.

Panhu
A magical dog that healed a queen and married a princess

The tale begins in an unnamed ancient Chinese kingdom in which the local queen suddenly fell ill. The royal doctors had no idea what was wrong with her and therefore could not help. It appeared that the queen might die, but an unknown deity intervened and set in motion a series of magical events. First, a gold-colored worm crawled from one of the queen's ears, after which she enjoyed a remarkable recovery. Next, the worm rapidly transformed into a cute, lovable dog.

The queen and the dog became inseparable, and she named him Panhu. He also proved useful to the kingdom. When the country went to war against a rival realm, Panhu killed the enemy king. That brought the conflict to a halt, after which everyone, including the queen, was shocked to hear Panhu speak. He boldly told her and the king that he wanted a reward for ending the war; namely, he aspired to marry their daughter. The king made it clear that they could not allow the princess to marry a mere dog, to which Panhu replied, "If that is all you are concerned about, please do as I ask. Place me beneath a golden bell."[24]

The royal couple agreed to grant this wish, and after sitting beneath the bell for a few days, the dog's body mutated into that of a muscular human male. His head remained canine, however. Nevertheless, the princess declared her love for Panhu, and the two were married. After that, in public she gladly donned furry hats so that they would look more alike. (Today some Chinese believe that they are Panhu's descendants and consider the mistreatment of dogs a sinful act.)

The Dragon King and Jade Emperor

Dogs appear in many stories from Chinese mythology, but they are not the most influential or the most prolific. The animals that fill those roles are dragons. In various stories, dragons either *are* gods or closely interact with the gods.

Nuwa was not the only deity who had dragon-like features, for instance. Another was Long Wang, the so-called Dragon King. Not only did he sometimes display dragon form, he also controlled the actions of many dragons, along with most sea creatures. Long Wang was "known for his fierce and aggressive personality," the online site Mythopedia explains. "He answered to no one except the Jade Emperor himself. [The Dragon King] lived in a beautiful sea palace with his [dragon] brothers and regularly feasted on a diet of precious gems and pearls. The brothers communicated telepathically and could understand one another perfectly without speaking a single word."[25]

The reason that Long Wang answered to the Jade Emperor was that the latter was both the most powerful god and the leader of all the Chinese divinities. The Jade Emperor was said to have begun as a human hero. Over time, however, he was deified, or transformed into a god. Thereafter he took on a growing number of crucial duties and powers, including dispenser of justice and controller of the weather.

The Four Flying Heroes

Several of the Jade Emperor's myths involve his relationships with dragons. In one of the most often cited of those tales, he clashed with the legendary and heroic Four Dragons—who by name were the Yellow Dragon, Black Dragon, Long Dragon, and Pearl Dragon. The incident began with a prolonged drought that brought famine and misery to large sectors of humanity. The four flying heroes felt bad for the humans and wondered why the Jade Emperor had allowed the drought to continue so long. Obtaining

Sculpted figures from a modern Chinese theme park interact in a scene from the popular myth in which one of the heroic Eight Immortals rides a dragon across the sea's surface.

The Dog That Saved Humanity

One of the more popular animal myths of ancient China features a dog that interacts with the gods and thereby changes the course of human history. The story begins shortly after a terrible flood wiped out all the rice and other crops. To avoid starvation, most people reverted to hunting wild game, but some families still had little to eat. One such family had a faithful and loving dog and made sure she was well fed despite their own hunger.

For that and other reasons, the dog loved her masters and yearned to help them. High up in heaven one of the gods detected that yearning and wanted to meet her. The deity raised the dog up into the divine realm of the Jade Emperor, and there the canine visitor saw that the gods had stored some seeds from rice, wheat, and other crops. She used body language and facial expressions to indicate her desire to bring the seeds back to earth. The gods could not resist her charm, so they gave her the seeds, and with them her masters and their neighbors began a second agricultural revolution. The ancient Chinese held that this story explained why so many people love and feel the need to protect and feed dogs.

an audience with that mighty deity, the dragons beseeched him to send heavy rains in order to save humankind.

The Jade Emperor at first sympathized with humanity's plight. He agreed to make it rain and thereby end the drought. Shortly after the dragons left his palace, however, the leading god became involved in another matter and forgot all about his promise to bring the needed rains. Several weeks passed, and the dragons could not understand why the king of heaven had not acted. Finally, they became fed up and determined to end the drought themselves. They promptly flew out over the ocean, scooped up millions of gallons of water, soared back over earth's surface, and dumped their precious payloads.

People everywhere sang hymns of praise for their deliverance from the catastrophe. But the Jade Emperor did not share in that elation. He was extremely unhappy that the dragons had made it rain behind his back, and he punished them by locking each in a cave inside a mountain. Fortunately for them—and in the long run, humanity—they possessed considerable magical abilities, and they employed them to bring up huge amounts of water

from deep underground. So plentiful were these flows that they formed China's greatest waterways—the Yellow, Black, Yangtze, and Pearl Rivers. Stunned by this feat, the Jade Emperor had a change of heart and thanked the flying heroes for creating a new and improved earthly landscape.

A Zoo of Popular Creatures

In addition to foxes, dogs, and dragons, many other animals played key roles in ancient Chinese myths. Those stories remain widely popular in modern China, where they are continually depicted in the arts and public media. As Ken Liu, a well-known translator of Chinese tales into English, puts it, "Chinese mythology has a rich menagerie of evocative creatures whose meanings have evolved over time and who are still being invoked and reinterpreted by Chinese writers, game designers, and filmmakers as part of the cultural conversation."[26]

Stories of a Wondrous Past: The Aztec Gods

Few of the residents of the splendid Toltecan city of Tollan noticed an unkempt little man wearing a torn tunic who arrived in the local marketplace one afternoon. He appeared to be a stranger. So a merchant asked him what he was doing in the realm's capital city. With a smile, the newcomer replied that he too was a merchant, Toueyo by name, and that he was looking for the royal palace.

After getting directions and reaching the royal residence, Toueyo approached a guard and asked to see the king's daughter. Surprised, the sentry only laughed. Why would the princess care to speak with a lowly merchant? he asked. No sooner had those words left his lips than five more guards appeared from inside the palace, followed by the princess herself. The young woman was on her way to shop in the marketplace. But the moment she locked eyes with Toueyo, her whole demeanor changed. Suddenly, she declared that she was in love with the ragged little merchant.

What neither the princess nor the guards realized was that Toueyo was not a merchant. Nor was he even human. Rather, he was the fierce and mean-spirited god of fate and

war, Tezcatlipoca, in disguise. He was an-
noyed that a fellow deity whom he hated
had brought peace and prosperity to the
Toltecs and desired to reverse that situation. As part of his plan
to punish his divine rival, Tezcatlipoca had cast a spell on the
princess. Her father, the king of the Toltecs, suspected something
was amiss but could not figure out exactly what. So the monarch
decided to save his daughter by finding a way to kill Toueyo.

It was too late, however. The still-disguised deity secretly sent
messages far and wide that a huge celebration would take place
in Tollan in honor of the princess's impending wedding. As a result, a few days later massive crowds formed in the city's main
square, and people sang and danced and feasted.

At the height of the festivities, Tezcatlipoca sprang his trap.
With a wave of his hand, he caused the assembled people to
dance with ever-increasing speed. "Faster and faster the people
danced," wrote the late mythologist Lewis Spence, "until the pace
became so furious that they were driven to madness." The crazed
Toltecs "lost their footing," Spence went on, "and tumbled pell-
mell down a deep ravine, where they were changed into rocks.
Others, in attempting to cross a stone bridge, [plunged] into the
water below, and were changed into stones."[27]

Larger-than-Life Past Peoples

This tale of the god Tezcatlipoca's jealousy and wrath was one of
the chief myths of the Mexica people, today better known as the
Aztecs. The Aztecs created a large empire in Central America between the 1300s and 1500s. Only part of that story was fanciful. The
people whose downfall was described in the myth—the Toltecs—
were very real. They had occupied the same region from the 900s to
1100s and built a complex civilization there, only to rapidly decline
and disappear long before the Aztecs came on the scene.

Several other Aztec myths involved the Toltecs, whom the Aztecs revered. According to Arizona State University scholar Michael E. Smith, "In the Aztec histories, the Toltecs of Tollan were

Dating from about 1500—at the height of the Aztecs' power and influence in central Mexico—this turquoise ceremonial mask depicts the formidable, often mean-spirited god of war, Tezcatlipoca.

idealized as great, wise, wealthy, and almost superhuman people. These histories claimed that the Toltecs invented all of the arts and crafts of [ancient Central America]."[28]

In fact, the Toltecs were not the only vanished people who played major roles in Aztec mythology and formed integral parts of the Aztecs' worldview. Other Central American civilizations that found their way into Aztec lore included those of the Olmecs, Zapotecs, and Teotihuacanos. The latter, for instance, had left behind the city of Teotihuacan, covering an astounding 8 square miles (20 sq. km). It contained over one hundred temples and other large structures, one of them towering to a height of 246 feet (75 m). The Aztecs viewed the deserted Teotihuacan as the sacred birthplace of the gods and made annual religious pilgrimages to that giant ghost town.

The Myth Behind Human Sacrifice

Many of the Aztec myths strongly influenced their social and religious customs. The tale of the sun and moon is one such myth. In the story, the newly formed earth had no sun. The deity Nanauatzin realized that crops would need sunlight to grow. So he sacrificed himself by jumping into a fire and afterwards rising up to become the sun. Not to be outdone, another god, Tecuciztecatl, did the same. For a short time, two suns shone in the daytime sky, casting too much sunlight on the land. To remedy the situation, a third divinity tossed a rabbit at Tecuciztecatl. His brightness dimmed, and he became the moon. At first, the sun and moon did not move. So the other gods jumped into the fire. The energy created by this action set the heavens in motion.

These deities were later reborn, but in sacrificing themselves they had performed what the Aztecs viewed as a heroic act. The belief was that humans owed the gods an immense debt, and the only way to properly repay it was for some humans to die each year as sacrifices to those divine beings. This, experts believe, was the origin of the periodic, bloody human sacrifices performed by Aztec priests.

Like other world mythologies, Aztec mythology included tales that described the gods, the world's creation, the natural elements, and the origins of various common social customs. For example, some Aztec myths describe how fire came from the god of light, Ometeotl; other stories mention the adventures of Mictlantecuhtli, who oversaw the underworld; and still others feature Tlaloc, the deity who brought rain.

Ometeotl
The Aztec deity of light and fire

Yet many of the stories that made up Aztec mythology also shared a common theme. That overarching idea was that the Aztecs themselves evolved from a wondrous past inhabited by larger-than-life peoples who had been blessed by the gods. Moreover, those past peoples were not legendary. Indeed, archaeologists have shown that all of them actually existed. The Aztecs saw themselves as the heirs of a glorious historical past and saw this special heritage as proof that the gods had chosen them to rule over other peoples.

Mictlantecuhtli
The god of the underworld, the dark realm of the dead

A Seemingly Endless Series of Battles

Among those ancient gods, Tezcatlipoca, the destroyer of the Toltecs, long remained one of the most feared and revered. His rival—the deity who had brought peace and prosperity to the Toltecs—was Quetzalcoatl, often called the Feathered Serpent. He was a major creator deity whom the Aztecs also saw as the god of healing and a protector of artists. In addition, he was thought to have been the Toltecs' first great ruler.

In a long series of myths describing the histories of past ages, with each age called a "sun" in the Aztec language, Quetzalcoatl and Tezcatlipoca battled each other. Each time one of them gained an advantage, the other found a way to get revenge. Moreover, each of the competing divinities created diverse and at times exotic races of humans and other creatures in efforts to defeat the other.

Another major Aztec myth about the rivalry between the two deities told how Tezcatlipoca pretended to befriend the Feathered Serpent and got him drunk.

Found in an old Aztec religious manuscript, this stunning painting shows the god Quetzalcoatl—the so-called Feathered Serpent (at left)—confronting his enemy and fellow deity, Tezcatlipoca.

That disgraced Quetzalcoatl in the eyes of the Toltecs, so he chose to exile himself. In some versions of the tale, he promised he would return someday. That became a prophecy that many Aztecs later believed to be fulfilled in real life. When the Spaniards, led by military adventurer Hernan Cortes, invaded Mexico in 1519, the Aztec king Motecuhzoma suspected that Cortes was the returning Quetzalcoatl.

Journey to a New Homeland

The history of a drama-filled past age was also the central theme of perhaps the most important of all the Aztec myths involving gods—the story of the Aztecs' own origins. They themselves acknowledged that they did not evolve in central Mexico but rather immigrated from somewhere else. Exactly where that homeland was remains somewhat uncertain to this day. But according to

A map dating from the 1700s shows a fanciful depiction of the mythical great migration, in which the Aztecs journeyed from their mysterious homeland of Aztlan to south-central Mexico.

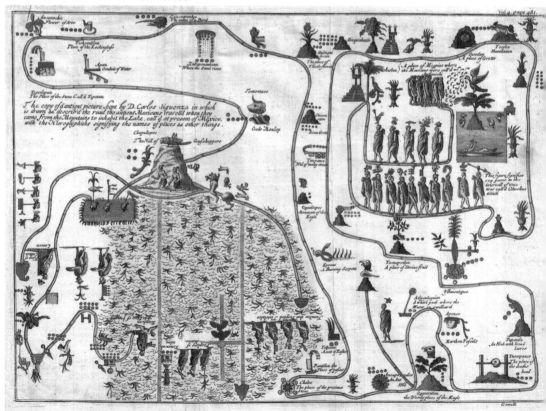

Where Was Aztlan?

In the lore of the Mexica/Aztecs, before their grand journey to the Valley of Mexico, they lived in a place called Aztlan. There they dwelled on an island floating in a large lake. Modern scholars have proposed a number of geographical regions where the historical Aztlan might have existed—if it actually did exist. North-central and east-central Mexico have both been candidates for that legendary land. A majority of experts favor a location farther north, however, in the southwestern United States. One clue supporting this view is that Nahuatl, the language the Aztecs spoke, has many similarities to the tongue spoken by a Native American people called the Ute, who held sway in Colorado and Utah. Kelley Hays-Gilpin, an archaeologist based at Northern Arizona University, thinks there may actually have been two major Aztec migrations. She suggests the Aztecs initially dwelled in central Mexico and over time moved northward into Arizona and Utah. Later, she says, they reversed themselves and journeyed southward, back into Mexico.

the myth, it was known as Aztlan, and it existed somewhere north of Mexico's central valley.

In that epic story, the Aztecs lived in Aztlan for unknown numbers of centuries and were content there because the weather was good, the soil fertile, and game plentiful. However, one cloudless day they heard a titanic thunderclap, and their patron deity, or national protector god, Huitzilopochtli appeared in the town square of the largest Aztec town. Addressing the people, he told them that they must soon pack their belongings, leave their homeland, and strike out toward the south.

The great migration lasted many decades because the Aztecs stopped from time to time to plant and harvest crops to sustain themselves. Eventually, though, they

Huitzilopochtli
The Aztecs' patron god

moved on, trying to remain obedient to their divine patron. In that regard, the Aztec priests said that they often received messages from Huitzilopochtli, who ordered them to continue southward. In time, he said, they would behold a visual sign that would show them they had reached their new home. More specifically, they would see a giant eagle standing above a cactus imbedded in a big rock. There, the god stated, the Aztecs' "name will be praised and our Aztec nation made great. The might of our arms will be known and the courage of our brave hearts." He added, "There we will build the city . . . [and] rule over all others."[29]

In the fullness of time, these prophetic words came true. The migrating Aztecs arrived in the fertile Valley of Mexico. Most of the peoples who then occupied the region were hostile to the newcomers. So the Aztecs ended up wandering along the shores of the vast inland sea known as Lake Texcoco. It was while they were rounding the lake's southern rim that they witnessed the fulfillment of Huitzilopochtli's prophecy. Some official Aztec scribes later recorded that the people encountered a tall cactus seemingly growing out of a big rock. Moreover, perched atop the cactus was

> an eagle with its wings extended toward the rays of the sun, taking its heat in the coolness of the morning. [When] they saw it, [they] bowed down in reverence, [while] the eagle, when he saw them, bowed down, lowering his head. . . . [The Aztec leaders proclaimed,] "We have attained what we were searching for, and we have found our city and site, thanks to the Lord of Creation and to our god Huitzilopochtli."[30]

Centuries later, in the 1900s the Republic of Mexico adopted a national flag showing an eagle sitting on a cactus growing from a rock. Many of those who chose that image for the flag were descendants of the Spaniards who destroyed the Aztec nation centuries before. The flag's adoption was partly viewed as a sort of apology for that long-ago conquest. It was also seen as a recognition that the Aztecs' mixture of myth and history helped make Mexican culture possible. As one expert observer puts it, "The Mexican flag waving over Mexico is a powerful reminder of the rich history carried forward from the bygone era. It signifies the transformation from being the Aztecs of Tenochtitlan to growing as the proud Mexican citizens. When the citizens of Mexico pledge their allegiance to the Mexican flag, they can pride themselves on being a part of a nation with a great heritage."[31]

Heaven's Vast Spirit Army: The Igbo Gods

One day Chukwu, the exalted high god of western Africa's Igbo (or Ibo) people, decided it was time for a major change. For untold centuries—ever since creating the world, including humans—he had been an extremely approachable deity. He had spent some time in heaven each year but had also made regular visits to earth. There, people of all walks of life frequently searched him out and asked him questions, and most of the time—no matter how seemingly inconsequential—he obligingly answered them. In the words of University of Massachusetts professor Chukwuma Azuonye, "Everyone who lost his kitchen knife would go to Chukwu to inquire why it was lost; everyone who lost his tapping knife [used to extract tree sap] would go to Chukwu to inquire why and how it was lost; anybody who lost his tapping rope [used to hold the sap collection bowl] would go to inquire from Chukwu why it was lost. And he would be told why."[32]

The problem was that there seemed to be no limits to the demands made upon Chukwu every day of the week, and he steadily grew tired of his own notoriety. A god should have a certain amount of time to himself, he decided. So the mighty deity who largely controlled all that existed suddenly withdrew from the earthly scene and made heaven his permanent abode.

As for the humans who worshipped Chukwu, they learned to pray to him when they wanted answers to their questions. Such conversations were now one-sided, as he no longer answered each question individually. Instead, he assigned intermediaries, or go-betweens, to receive the questions and provide the answers. Some of those representatives of heaven were human priests. But most were either divine spirits Chukwu had created or the spirits of human ancestors. In this way, the chief god made religion far more complex and regimented than it had been in the past.

Regular Sacrifices to the Spirits

The story about how Chukwu stopped communing directly with people and transferred that duty to a vast spirit army is one of many myths associated with that leading god of the Igbo pantheon. The age of that and other Igbo myths is unknown, but most modern experts think they are extremely old. Indeed, abundant archaeological evidence shows that the Igbo have dwelled in what is now Nigeria and surrounding regions for at least two thousand years, and the earliest vestiges of Igbo culture may be up to a millennium older than that.

During all those centuries, there was ample time for Chukwu to evolve from an easily accessible deity to a faraway and mysterious one. As for why he became so shadowy, all the Igbo knew was contained in the myth of his withdrawal from earth and appointment of intermediaries between himself and humanity. According to Don C. Ohadike, a noted scholar of Igbo culture, the

Chukwu
The chief god of the Igbo pantheon

Igbo people of medieval and early modern times "nursed a deep reverence for the mysterious nature of Chukwu. They were not sure how to approach him, but they knew that he was a spirit and that those who worshiped him must do so in

This modern puppet of the chief Igbo god Chukwu is made of leather and wood. According to Igbo mythology, in the dimly remembered past that deity created the world and its contents.

spirit. They therefore communed with him through the major spirits and ancestors."[33]

People were also expected to make regular sacrifices to those many nature spirits and spirits of human ancestors, says Congolese scholar E. Elochukwu Uzukwu. Most often those sacrifices took the form of animals such as goats or cows, he explains. "Sacrifices at fixed times of the year normally came at planting and harvest seasons." Those gestures to the spirits, along with prayers, Uzukwu points out, "show us that the Igbo considered the union or communion with Chukwu [and] ancestors and spirits as absolutely vital in their universe. Without these, life can neither be maintained nor augmented [made better]."[34]

Ahiajioku's Divine Transformation

Some of the Igbo myths suggest that in ancient times, people also sacrificed humans to Chukwu and other divine beings. One of the most important of these stories was one that told how the custom of growing crops originated. The tale also explains how the son of the principal character, Eri, became the god of agriculture.

Eri was an Igbo farmer who, like other food producers of his day, suffered greatly during a famine caused by a severe drought. Also like his fellow farmers, Eri worried so much about the crisis

Ahiajioku
A farmer's son who became the Igbo god of agriculture

that he prayed to Chukwu and begged the high god to intervene and bring rain to end the dry spell. Soon, speaking through an angel-like spirit go-between, Chukwu agreed to that request but attached a condition to it. Namely, he demanded that Eri sacrifice his eldest son, Ahiajioku, as well as his daughter Ada. Their deaths, the god's representative stated, would have the beneficial effect of saving thousands of other children from starvation.

After Eri's two offspring were slain, the spirit told Eri, he should slice their bodies into dozens of pieces and bury them in mounds of earth. In time, yam and palm trees and various vegetables would grow up from those mounds, and enough food would be produced to halt hunger among the starving Igbo people. Moreover, the angel said, the yam would become the symbol of young Ahiajioku, whose own spirit would thereafter be the deity of both yams and agriculture in general.

After Eri killed his son and daughter, yam trees grew up from their gravesites. This Igbo carving is dedicated to Kwale, the divine protector of the yam, a vegetable similar to a sweet potato.

Ahiajioku's Transformation

Many of the Igbo myths had a strong influence on ancient, medieval, and early modern Igbo culture. One of the more popular examples was the tale of Ahiajioku's transformation from an ordinary person into the god of agriculture. Each year in early August, during the New Yam Festival, people reenacted key sections of the myth. Typically, a person playing the role of the farmer Eri placed four or eight new yams on the ground near a shrine. The person recited a prayer and then sliced off some thin pieces of each yam, an act that symbolized Ahiajioku's body being cut into dozens of separate pieces. The yams were then cooked with palm oil, water, and strips of chicken—producing a meal that represented the body and blood of Ahiajioku. The reenactment of the myth honored the memory of Eri and Ahiajioku. It also reminded people that the hard work and industry displayed by early farmers like Eri was mirrored by the good work ethic of the Igbo people as a whole. In addition to this society-wide annual festival, individual farmers regularly offered animal sacrifices to Ahiajioku, hoping that doing so would convince the gods to guarantee a bountiful harvest.

The Penalty for Disobedience

Both yams and spirits play central roles in another old Igbo myth involving food. In that tale, a young, physically attractive girl named Obaledo learned that her parents were planning a journey to visit relatives in a distant village. While they were away, they told her, she was to stay home and take care of the family hut and her younger siblings. The parents also left an ample supply of yams and snails for the children to eat and instructed Obaledo to always cook the yams first, *before* the snails. If she roasted the snails first, they explained, the juices from those creatures would extinguish the fire, which would thereafter be difficult to rekindle. After Obaledo's father and mother departed, she initially followed their instructions to the letter. But by the second day she felt the taste of the snails irresistible and decided to disobey her parents and cook the snails first. Sure enough, the fire went out, just as the parents had foretold it would. Reasoning that a lit torch would quickly remedy the situation, the girl went to a neighbor's house in hopes of borrowing a torch. Thus, she left the house unattended, thereby disobeying her parents a second time.

Unfortunately for Obaledo, in Igbo lore the many existing spirits, including the souls of deceased ancestors, kept a close eye on people and their actions. So the girl's defiance of her parents did not go unnoticed. While she headed for the neighbor's house, one of the spirits who followed her happened to be a demon, and he decided to punish her. The nasty spirit snatched away the girl's natural beauty, and she remained ugly for the rest of her days.

How Death Became Permanent

In cultures that have been shaped by Jewish, Christian, and Muslim faiths, demons are usually thought to be evil and often vengeful entities. This is not the case in Igbo culture. In most versions of the tale about Obaledo, the demon does not rob the girl of her beauty out of spite or wickedness. Rather, in ancient Igbo eyes it was Obaledo who committed an evil act when she disobeyed her parents, and the demon had a duty to punish her.

In fact, to the Igbo a common belief was that the existence of an inherently evil spirit reflected badly on the great god Chukwu, who was innately good and created only good things. In contrast, evil stemmed only from humans and their own actions, according to Nigerian philosophy professors Babajide Dasaolu and Demilade Oyelakun. People themselves are "therefore responsible for every evil that happens in this world because of their actions and mode of being in the Igbo world. This view consolidates the African notion of evil that God can never be the proximate [immediate] cause of evil in the world."[35]

Similarly, permanent death, which is often portrayed as negative in Western society, did not initially exist in the world according to Igbo mythology. Instead, in the years immediately following the creation, Chukwu disliked the concept of the finality of death for his human creations. So he sent a talking dog to deliver a mes-

The Earth Mother Goddess

As high god, Chukwu was revered by the Igbo people, but he was not the only god they held in their hearts. Ala (or Ani), a female deity fashioned by Chukwu during the creation, was much loved by the people. She was the great mother goddess of the earth itself. (Her name literally translates as the word *ground* in the Igbo language.) Every Igbo home had a small shrine dedicated to Ala, and family members prayed to her daily. The remote place where she supposedly dwelled was often pictured as a sort of underworld. The spirits of virtuous dead people were said to flow toward her and ultimately rest within her great body, in some accounts inside her womb. (The spirits of bad people were thought to simply rot away in remote deserts or forests.) In addition, Ala was the deity of morality, and in that role she judged the rightness or wrongness of human actions. It was also thought that she unleashed hordes of army ants on wrongdoers as a punishment.

sage to the residents of the first human villages. The message was that if people covered their dead in ashes and buried them, the bodies would rise up and live forever.

The problem was that on his way to the villages, the dog got distracted by an opportunity for a meal and never delivered the message. On learning that, Chukwu next sent a talking sheep on this same errand. However, the sheep had trouble remembering what it was told and forgot to deliver the message. Mighty Chukwu, still relying on go-betweens to communicate with his human creations, tried several other animal messengers, but for various reasons all failed in their mission. The great god became frustrated and gave up on the project. As a result, death became permanent. "In Igbo mythology," therefore, state Nigerian scholars Amarachi Nnachi Ukoma and Uka-Egwu Roseline Onyinyech, "death is a respectful end. This is shown during burial where the dead are treated with utmost dignity."[36]

As has been true in human cultures around the globe, Igbo myths provided people with explanations of the many mysteries that filled their lives. The stories they told and retold, passing from one generation to the next, helped shape the customs and beliefs that guided their world.

Introduction: Miraculous Births and Other World Myths

1. Hesiod, *Theogony* 923–26, trans. Don Nardo.
2. E.J. Michael Witzel, *The Origins of the World's Mythologies*. New York: Oxford University Press, 2012, pp. 2–3.
3. Witzel, *The Origins of the World's Mythologies*, p. 75.
4. Witzel, *The Origins of the World's Mythologies*, p. 419.

Chapter One: Immortality and Power: The Greco-Roman Gods

5. Quoted in Theoi Greek Mythology, "Athene Myths 1." www.theoi.com.
6. Pindar, *Odes*, in C.M. Bowra, trans., *Pindar: The Odes*. New York: Penguin, 1985, p. 206.
7. W.H.D. Rouse, *Gods, Heroes and Men of Ancient Greece*. New York: New American Library, 2001, p. 18.
8. Quoted in Theoi Greek Mythology, "Ovid, Fasti 1." www.theoi.com.
9. Virgil, *Aeneid*, trans. Patric Dickinson. New York: New American Library, 2002, pp. 10–11.
10. Quoted in Theoi Greek Mythology, "Ovid, Fasti 6." www.theoi.com.
11. Jane F. Gardner, *Roman Myths*. Austin: University of Texas Press, 1993, p. 55.

Chapter Two: Trade-Offs and Tragedy: The Norse Gods

12. Christian Christensen, "This Is Why Odin Sacrificed His Eye," Scandinavia Facts, 2020. https://scandinaviafacts.com.

13. Edith Hamilton, *Mythology*. New York: Grand Central, 1999, p. 300.
14. Hamilton, *Mythology*, pp. 308–09.
15. Neil Philip, *The Illustrated Book of Myths, Tales, and Legends of the World*. New York: Dorling Kindersley, 1995, p. 67.
16. Philip, *The Illustrated Book of Myths, Tales, and Legends of the World*, p. 67.
17. Henry A. Bellows, trans., *Voluspo*, Sacred Texts. www.sacred-texts.com.

Chapter Three: Eternity and Endless Cycles: The Hindu Gods

18. Quoted in Ananda Garden, "Hymn to Brahma." https://anandagarden.com.
19. Veronica Ions, *Indian Mythology*. New York: Peter Bedrick, 1984, p. 24.
20. *The Ramayana*, trans. Hari P. Shastri, ed. Elizabeth Seeger. New York: William R. Scott, 1969, pp. 212–13.
21. Sadhguru, "Krishna Stories: Exploring Krishna's Path of the Playful," August 25, 2016. https://isha.sadhguru.org.
22. Subhamoy Das, "Vehicles of the Hindu Gods: The Vahanas," Learn Religions, 2019. www.learnreligions.com.

Chapter Four: Foxes, Dogs, and Dragons: The Chinese Gods

23. Tao Tao Liu Sanders, *Dragons, Gods, and Spirits from Chinese Mythology*. New York: Peter Bedrick, 1994, pp. 15–16.
24. Quoted in Sanders, *Dragons, Gods, and Spirits from Chinese Mythology*, p. 39.
25. Mae Hamilton, "Dragon King," Mythopedia, 2019. https://mythopedia.com.
26. Ken Liu, "5 Chinese Mythological Creatures That Need to Appear in More SF/F," *Sci-Fi & Fantasy* (blog), Barnes & Noble, April 12, 2016. www.barnesandnoble.com.

Chapter Five: Stories of a Wondrous Past: The Aztec Gods

27. Lewis Spence. "Chapter II: Mexican Mythology," Sacred Texts. www.sacred-texts.com.

28. Michael E. Smith, "Toltec Empire," Academia, 2016. www .academia.edu.
29. Quoted in Fray Diego Duran, *The History of the Indies of New Spain*, trans. Doris Heyden. Norman: University of Oklahoma Press, 1994, pp. 43–44.
30. Quoted in Eduardo M. Moctezuma, "Aztec History and Cosmovision," in *Moctezuma's Mexico: Visions of the Aztec World*, ed. David Carrasco and Eduardo M. Moctezuma. Niwot: University Press of Colorado, 1992, p. 19.
31. Prakrite, "The Mexican Flag—History & Meaning," Rover-Atlas, February 4, 2020. https://roveratlas.com.

Chapter Six: Heaven's Vast Spirit Army: The Igbo Gods

32. Chukwuma Azuonye, "Igbo Folktales and the Idea of Chukwu as the Supreme God of Igbo Religion," University of Massachusetts, Boston, April 1987, p. 47.
33. Don C. Ohadike, "Igbo Culture and History," in *Things Fall Apart*, ed. Chinua Achebe. Portsmouth, NH: Heinemann, 1996, p. xxxiii.
34. E. Elochukwu Uzukwu, "Igbo World and Ultimate Reality and Meaning," University of Toronto Press Journals, 2020. www .utpjournals.press.
35. Babajide Dasaolu and Demilade Oyelakun, "The Concept of Evil in Yoruba and Igbo Thoughts: Some Comparisons," Philosophia, 2015. https://philosophia-bg.com.
36. Amarachi Nnachi Ukoma and Uka-Egwu Roseline Onyinyech, "Igbo Cosmology: The Concept of Death as a Means to Final Rest," *IDOSR Journal of Current Issues in Arts and Humanities* 4, no. 1, 2018, p. 24.

Books

Matt Clayton, *Hindu Mythology*. Charleston, SC: Amazon Digital Services, 2018.

Tammy Gagne, *Chinese Gods, Heroes, and Mythology*. Minneapolis, MN: ABDO, 2019.

Katerina Servi, *Greek Mythology: Gods & Heroes—the Trojan War and the* Odyssey. Baton Rouge, LA: Third Millennium, 2018.

David Stuttard, *Roman Mythology: A Traveler's Guide from Troy to Tivoli*. London: Thames and Hudson, 2019.

Isabel Wyatt, *Norse Myths and Viking Legends*. Edinburgh, Scotland: Floris, 2020.

Internet Sources

Subhamoy Das, "10 of the Most Important Hindu Gods," ThoughtCo, 2019. www.thoughtco.com.

Ducksters, "Ancient China: Mythology," 2019. www.ducksters.com.

Hinduwebsite.com, "Brahman: The Supreme Self," 2019. www.hinduwebsite.com.

Léonie Chao-Fong, "The 8 Most Important Gods and Goddesses of the Aztec Empire," 2020. www.historyhit.com.

Greek Travel Tellers, "Meet the Olympian Gods," 2020. https://greektraveltellers.com.

E. Elochukwu Uzukwu, "Igbo World and Ultimate Reality and Meaning," University of Toronto Press Journals, 2020. www.utp journals.press.

Donald L. Wasson, "Roman Mythology," Ancient History Encyclopedia, 2018. www.ancient.eu.

Kuan L. Yong, "108 Chinese Mythological Gods and Characters to Know About," Owlcation, September 9, 2020. https://owl cation.com.

Websites

Chinese Mythology, Godchecker (www.godchecker.com /chinese-mythology). Conceived by the late modern mythologist Chas Saunders, this informational site explains the best-known ancient Chinese gods in a well-designed, eye-catching format.

Hinduism, History (www.history.com/topics/religion/hinduism). One of the two or three best overall websites on the internet about Hinduism, this offers the basic facts behind Hindu gods, beliefs, sacred writings, rituals, and much more.

Theoi Greek Mythology (www.theoi.com). This is the most comprehensive and reliable general website about Greek mythology on the internet. It features hundreds of separate pages filled with detailed, accurate information, as well as numerous primary sources and reproductions of ancient paintings and mosaics.